# 21 DAY SPIRITUAL

## MEDITATION JOURNAL

**Syrena N. Williams**

21 Day Spiritual Meditation Journal


Cover design by Dr. Susan James
Cover photography by Syd Williams
Quilt on cover by Dr. Michelle Howard Harrell
Back photo by Elizabeth Ashley & Co.



To contact the publisher, visit
www.PracticalSkillsU.com
To contact the author, visit
www.PracticalSkillsU.com

ISBN: 978-0-578-84805-1

# FOREWARD

From my very first personal encounter with Syrena, I understood the calling placed on her life to minister to and meet the needs of others. Her unique spiritual gifts give her the ability to discern what is needed, her compassion gives her the ability to meet people where they are, and her professional and educational experiences give her the wisdom to provide wise counsel.

Syrena has been an amazing prayer partner and friend. We have grown together as friends and in our spiritual journey. I can always count on her to get me out of my own head and steer me back to God. I was so delighted when she told me she would be publishing this book of meditations. I have had the awesome privilege of participating in her live meditation every Thursday evening. Weekly meditation really has provided me with the time and space to **STOP** and **BREATHE**. If you live busy schedules overflowing with lists of things to get done, as most of us do, you know the importance of being able to do those two things. Usually, by Thursday, I am physically, mentally, and emotionally spent. When I complete our weekly meditation, it rejuvenates and empowers me. Any time you are in the presence of Godly sisters sharing and spending time focusing on targeted life-application scripture references, it changes the trajectory of your outlook. It feels like God steps right into your business and replaces your thoughts with His.

Some of the most powerful and impactful meditations for me have been *Expecting God to crown my year with his bounty* (Ps. 65.11); *Seeking God for miracles* (Job 5:9); and that *I am perfect just as I am* (Ps 139:13-14) just to name a few. There is no other place that you can find yourself and lose yourself at the same time. Spiritual meditation is it!! That is a new level of encouragement! In hindsight, I always thought I was not one for meditation until now.

Today as I write the foreword to this Spiritual Meditation Journal, I am convinced that if you follow through this 21-day meditation journey, it will be life-changing. Just as Syrena captivates me with her spiritual and professional insight, you, too, will now know how wonderful it is to be blessed by such an amazing author. I just have the privilege of calling her, my sister.

Enjoy!

Paula Finley

# Intro

Welcome to this 21-Day guided spiritual journey! It is my pleasure to assist you with meditating on God's word. It is my heart's desire that through this journey, you will draw closer to God, love yourself more, and begin to love others better.

Now, please realize that there is no right way to go through this book! It is laid out in a way to let you know what each meditation is about. However, it is up to you to get in tune with yourself and choose what you need each day. Read them in whatever order makes sense to you. Give yourself time to do the journal pieces to further deepen your meditation.

I have placed "Why Meditate" first and then listed all others in alphabetical order. "Why Meditate" seems like a good place to start if you are a beginner to meditation, if you are wondering why this meditation includes scripture or if you want to prepare your mind for this journey. So, with that being said, it's your bonus meditation! There are actually 22 meditations in this book.

I will be praying for each person that has this book in their hand, that you will have an open heart and mind during the next few days; that you will create some type of meditation routine (daily, weekly, monthly, etc.), and that you will share what you learn with others and spread the good news of the Lord!

Peace, Blessings, and Joy!

# Meditations

# Why Meditate

**Finally, brethren, whatever things are true, whatever things are noble, whatever things are just, whatever things are pure, whatever things are lovely, whatever things are of good report, if there is any virtue and if there is anything praiseworthy—meditate on these things. The things which you learned and received and heard and saw in me, these do, and the God of peace will be with you. – Philippians 4: 8-10 (NIV)**

**Keep this Book of the Law always on your lips; meditate on it day and night so that you may be careful to do everything written in it. Then you will be prosperous and successful. – Joshua 1:8 (NIV)**

Find a comfortable position
Begin to focus on your breathing
Allow yourself to relax
Follow your breath with your mind

Take a deep breath in with your nose
Feel your breath go in your nose
Down your throat
Expand your chest
Open up your hips
Revive your thighs
Tingle your calves and
Tickle your toes

As you exhale
Feel the release of all negative things leaving every inch of your body
and flying out of your mouth

Breathe slowly
Continue to breathe at a pace that allows you to remain comfortable and at ease

Find a moment to clear your mind
Declutter any thoughts floating around
Acknowledge the thoughts that come up and then dismiss them from this space
When outside thoughts arise, refocus on your breathing

Focus on what is noble in your life
Focus on things in your life that are pure
Focus on what is lovely in your life
Focus on things that are good
Good things continue to happen to you regardless of your actions
Focus on God's grace in your life
Focus on God's forgiveness
Focus on God's abundant blessings

Breathe in God's peace
Exhale all anxieties

Inhale God's wisdom
Exhale all doubts

Inhale God's goodness
Exhale all bad thoughts

Inhale God's light
Exhale every inch of darkness in your body

Inhale God's perfection
Exhale every imperfection you believe exists in your body

Inhale God's compassion
Exhale all judgments

Focus on your rhythm of breathing

Focus on how you are feeling and grant yourself permission to feel however it is

When you are ready
Prepare yourself in faith and go out in love to serve the Lord

## Journal Exercise:

1 – Write the things that were revealed to you during this meditation.

______________________________________________

______________________________________________

______________________________________________

2 – What can you do to re-focus your attention to these things several times during the day?

______________________________________________

______________________________________________

______________________________________________

3 – What is one thing you can do to improve your meditation practice?

______________________________________________

______________________________________________

______________________________________________

# A New Guarded Heart

**Above all else, guard your heart, for everything you do flows from it. – Proverbs 4:23 (NIV)**
**I will give you a new heart and put a new spirit in you. I will remove from you your heart of stone and give you a heart of flesh. – Ezekiel 36:26 (NIV)**

Find a place where you can settle in and be comfortable
That can be seated
lying down
or standing up
Whatever provides you with comfort right now

We are going to start with our breathing
If you are in a place where you can hold your hands open and up please do
We are going to invite in the Holy Spirit and God's energy as we are breathing

If you are not in a place to hold your hands up
it is quite okay
God knows how to get to us

Breathe in through your nose for 2 counts
Breathe out for 4 counts through our mouths

On the second breath in
purposefully expand your stomach and chest
and see if you can follow the breath in your body

As you exhale
feel the air leaving your body coming up from your stomach
and feel your stomach going back towards your back as your lungs decompress
and the breath goes out of your mouth

Feel the difference of weight in your head
Feel the lightheadedness

Take another deep breath in
Allow the breath to penetrate down through your lungs, hips, thighs and toes

Exhale releasing all stress and tensions

On the last breath in
Take a deep breath in to be cleansing
Invite the Holy Spirit in to stay and sit for a while

As we breathe out release anything not of God
Anything that is not supposed to be there

As we center our mind on the word
Think about the heart

Focus and settle your breathing to see if you can feel your heart
Are you able to feel it beating?
Are you able to feel the pulse vibrations that it sends through your body?
Is it beating fast or slow?
Has the rhythm changed with your breathing?
As we picture the heart
It is a small organ that God has so perfectly designed
to pump and keep this body, 100 times its size, going
Going all-day
As we think about the heart
The blood flows into it
The blood flows out of it
If the block is not clean, it can clog the arteries

It will have to work harder
It can even stop the beating
As we think about the cleansing... the blood
Think about what do you put into your body that contaminates the blood
Too many sugars
Too many carbs
Alcohol
Drugs
Think about the Spirit and God cleansing our heart and putting into us a new heart
What are we putting into our Spirit that has clogged our spiritual arteries?
That might cause our spiritual heart to stop beating
That might cause our heart to be stone
Is it
Deceit
Jealousy
Envy
Boastfulness
Hatred
Sharp tongues
Favoritism
Non-invitation to the Holy Spirit
How are we creating the impurities that need to be cleansed?
As we praise God for his grace and mercies
To cleanse us because of no deeds of our own
To create new hearts in us when there is nothing we can do worthy to earn it
All He requires us to do is ask to be cleansed
And for us to continually guard our hearts

Pause and give thanks

Pause and praise him for the cleansing process

Pause and thank him for the gift of the heart of flesh
That produces love
That produces gentleness and kindness

That is a place where the Holy Spirit loves to be invited to and wants to stay all-day

I invite you to take in a deep breath through your nose
Exhaling through your mouth
As you do place your hand over your heart

Take in your second, breathe in and out
Ask God to cleanse your heart

Take in the next breath in and out
Guard your heart
This new one
Made of flesh
Not stone

When you are ready
Return to your surroundings

## Journal Exercise:

1 – How will you guard your heart?

______________________________________________

______________________________________________

______________________________________________

2 – What is flowing from your heart?

______________________________________________

______________________________________________

______________________________________________

3 – What is hidden in your heart?

______________________________________________

______________________________________________

______________________________________________

# Collaboration

**Two are better than one, because they have a good return for their labor: If either of them falls down, one can help the other up. But pity anyone who falls and has no one to help them up. – Ecclesiastes 4:9-10 (NIV)**
**When pride comes, then comes disgrace, but with humility comes wisdom. – Proverbs 11:2 (NIV)**

I invite you to get comfortable wherever you are
Find a place where you will have the least distractions
Increase your attention on the Lord
Prepare to focus on God's word today

We will meditate on the above verses and on collaboration

As we settle in
I ask you to take a few deep breaths
to cleanse your thoughts and minds and
get your blood flowing to all parts of your body intentionally

Take a deep breath in through your nose, slowly for two counts
Exhale through your mouth, breathing even slower for four counts
pressing your stomach towards your back
and clearing your mind of the thoughts of today

And as we take our next breath in
I want you to allow the breath to come in slowly through your body
and see if you can trace it with your mind
and allow your stomach to expand
and blow up like a balloon and be filled with all the air

And as we exhale
breathing through our mouth
releasing any toxins
releasing any resistance
releasing any distractions in our body

As we take our last deep breath in
just inhale collaboration and the help of others

As we exhale
I ask you to release the idea of doing things alone

Settle in and think about God's word
Think about the beginning of creation
when God created Adam
And while it was a good creation
when He finished His work
He looked at him
and said he needs a helpmate

And while there were many animals on this earth
God determined none were right to be Adam's helper
only another human creation would be
And so, He created Eve
a helpmate

I want you to think about the word "helpmate"
One who joins in part of the team
assists with doing the task
What do you really think about the word "help" when you hear it?
Do societal and world views come up for you?
Do you see asking for help as a weakness?
Does it feel like you might be burdening someone else?
Does a thing for you, like pride, get in your way?
When God gives you a large task that you know will either be a huge undertaking for you or a project for two or more, how do you view it?
Do you quickly seek a helpmate?

Someone who will produce and return good labor with you
Someone to assist you when you are down
A person who may pray for you
Who may physically pick you up
Who might dust you off
Who might hold your hands up while you're tired

Or does pride get in the way, and the task becomes too much
Insurmountable
A mess
A disgrace
When we try to do it all alone and know, we can't

When we pray to God for help, do we recognize that He might actually send another human being to help us?

Collaboration…
How do you work with others?
How can you invite collaboration into your life, into all the things that God would have you do that requires a helpmate?
How can you humble yourself and be wise enough to know the task is too big for you alone?
How will you seek discernment?

I invite you to take a deep breath in through your nose
and bring in wisdom
As we exhale through our mouths
I ask you to exhale pride

On the next deep breath in
breathe in discernment

As we exhale
breathe out "superwoman" or "superman"

And on our final deep breath in,
I ask you to breathe in an attitude that welcomes a helpmate

Exhale all guilt and all feelings of being alone

When you are ready
Return to your surroundings

## Journal Exercise:

1 – When do you resist help?

_______________________________________________

_______________________________________________

_______________________________________________

2 – What do you need help with?

_______________________________________________

_______________________________________________

_______________________________________________

3 – How can you let others in?

_______________________________________________

_______________________________________________

_______________________________________________

# Creating a Legacy

**A good person leaves an inheritance for their children's children, but the sinner's wealth is stored up for the righteous. – Proverbs 13:22 (NIV)**

Please get where you need to be
in a comfortable position to enable you to set your mind on God's word today

Wherever you are
allow yourself to settle in

Whether you are seated or lying down
put your arms together with the palms of your hands facing each other in front of you

As you take a deep breath in
I want you to open your arms wide

Let your chest fill up, and as you exhale through your mouth
and press your hands back together

We are mocking the body

As we breathe in
open your hands
fill your chest with air
This should make you sit up a bit taller to expand and feel the air inside of you

As we exhale

put your hands back together in front of you
Your stomach should be going towards your back
it might even curve in a little bit

We're going to do that two more times
We're going to inhale
arms out
Exhale
arms in

Last time
Inhale expanding your body filling up with air
Exhale decompressing, exhaling all non-holy things

As we sit in this moment, I want you to think about God's plan
I want you to think about where you are today in your life
Where are you physically?
Where are you mentally?
Where are you spiritually?
And how did you get there?
What was your journey?
Certainly, we are not where we started
Prayerfully, we are spiritually stronger than we used to be
As we strengthen this relationship that we have with our Lord and Savior, what is the gift that we are leaving for our children and our children's children?
What are we telling them we believe?
What are we showing them with our actions?
Are we givers?
Do we give gifts of life to others by speaking positively over them, by encouraging them, by praying over them, by giving them God's words of encouragement?
Do we give our money and talents to those who don't have or are in need?
Do we pray in secret or in public?
Do we pray over more than our meals?
Do we pray on more than Sundays?
Do they know the Lord is first every single day of our lives?
What is the inheritance we are leaving them?

Is it a solid foundation?
Are we planning for our end, to leave them the things we have worked so hard for: a good name, a good reputation, memories of joy and kindness?
Are we leaving a legacy of goodness, the expectation for them to live up to being a child of God?
Do they know who they belong to?
Do they know whose they are and who they are?
Or are we finding it to be awkward: not the right timing, not inviting them to hear the gospel music because they want to listen to the hip-hop music? Not to watch the Christian movies because they want to watch the secular movies? And maybe we are too.
How are we aligning our actions to ensure that when we meet our Maker, we will see our children and our children's children?
How are we paving the road for this inheritance?

Now I ask you to take in a deep breath with your hands in front of you, and as they expand and your body fills with air, I'm going to ask God to fill you with the right words
As you exhale take away any discomfort, emptying your body with air and bringing your hands together in front of you

As we inhale again, ask God to fill us with the right songs
And as we exhale, release all doubts and fears

As you inhale again, ask God to fill you with goodness and joy and His words, His scripture  And as you exhale, release any feeling of not giving in

When you are ready
Return to your surroundings

## Journal Exercise:

1 – How can you invite God into your relationships with your children and grandchildren?

________________________________________________________________

________________________________________________________________

________________________________________________________________

2 – What makes you hesitant to do so?

________________________________________________________________

________________________________________________________________

________________________________________________________________

3 – How can they lead the conversation?

________________________________________________________________

________________________________________________________________

________________________________________________________________

# Enriched Steps

**In their hearts, humans plan their course, but the Lord establishes their steps. – Proverbs 16:9 (NIV)**
**You will be enriched in every way so that you can be generous on every occasion, and through us, your generosity will result in thanksgiving to God. – 2 Corinthians 9:11**

I ask that you find a place that is comfortable for you
You can be seated
Kneeling
lying down
standing
whatever feels comfortable to you
Find a place where you can draw nearer to God

Let's take a few cleansing breaths
We're going to breathe in for two counts
and exhale through our mouths for four counts

As we take our first breath in through our nose
and exhale through our mouths
try to flatten your stomach towards your back
centering our thoughts on the Lord

Taking our second breath
Inhale
intentionally feeling the cool air enter our bodies
and exhale
feeling how in just seconds, we warm the air up

Keep focusing on God

And take another breath in
expanding our lungs
and exhaling
clarifying our thoughts on God's word

Steps...
We take our first steps as a toddler
and that's when we put one foot in front of the other
and we may be moving forward or backward
but it's a step

And then we learn to know there are things that hinder our steps
That's where we have surfaces that move from one level to the next
rising from one floor to another
Oftentimes, we learn in sports or games or processes
about taking steps to shift us into a new position

The Lord establishes our steps
the way we move forward
backward
from side to side
placing one foot in front of another

God establishes our steps
how we move from one level to the next
from one position to another position

He enriches us in every way
He improves our quality
He enhances our value
He makes us wealthier in mind, body, and spirit
And when he enriches our steps
He elevates us

I want you to imagine where you are right now in your life
What steps did God have you take to get there?
How were you sharpened during the process?
How were you refined on the path that He had you take?

How did He elevate you from one level to the next?
How did God enrich your steps?

Now that you have thought about what it took to get you here…
What will it take for you to trust God and move in your very next step?
What muscles do you need to grow and strengthen to take the next step?
Is it a physical muscle?
Is it a spiritual muscle?
Is it a mental muscle?

If we think about all the steps that God has for us
we wouldn't be able to see the top from the bottom
and we might not be able to see the bottom from the top
It's quite a journey
It's one where He stays with us from beginning to end
Where He pushes us to the limits, we didn't even know we had
Where He picks us up when we fall
and sometimes carries us to the finish line.

All so we can say thank you, God

How has our God enriched your steps?

I invite you to take a deep breath in through your nose
and breathe out through your mouth

This time when you breathe in through your nose
on your exhale, I want you to roll your shoulders back as you exhale

Last time, in through your nose
and out through your mouth
allowing yourself to let those breaths make a sound

When you are ready
Return to your surroundings

## Journal Exercise:

1 – What in your past seemed like a challenge but turned out to be a step?

______________________________________________

______________________________________________

______________________________________________

2 – In what way has God enriched you so that you are able to be generous to others?

______________________________________________

______________________________________________

______________________________________________

# Fall in Love With God

**Trust in the Lord with all your heart and lean not on your own understanding; in all your ways, submit to him, and he will make your paths straight. – Proverbs 3:5-6 (NIV)**

Find a comfortable place
Sit, stand, lay down
get wherever you can to be still for a moment

Breathe in, taking a moment to declutter your mind
Breathe out, exhaling all distractions

Breathe in and out, slowly finding a rhythm where you can relax

Follow your breath in and out

Finding a place in your mind where you can just be in there – just you and God

When is the last time you gave God all of you?
Your thoughts
Your actions
Your words
Your entire heart

Imagine falling in love with God
Attending to him the way he attends to you
Learning all the intimate things about him

What makes him smile?
Learning his decrees to honor him

What makes him proud?
Trusting and obeying him

How does he like to be praised?
In song
With trumpets
With harps
With lyre
With cymbals
Clapping your hands and shouting

What does he want to be for you?
A confidant
A consultant
A provider
A healer
A creator
A supplier
My peace
A comforter
Giver of wisdom
My strength

Imagine loving God as he loves you
Envision him truly being the most important thing in your life

Breathe in and receive his love
Exhale any doubt of his ability to love you

Breathe in alignment
Exhale anything getting you off track

Allow yourself the time to you need to embrace all that you have seen
and heard during this exercise

When you are ready
Return to your surroundings

## Journal Exercise:

1 – In what ways can I tend to God daily to show him that he is all those things to me?

______________________________________________

______________________________________________

______________________________________________

2 – How can I make room for God to live in me and be comfortable?

______________________________________________

______________________________________________

______________________________________________

3 – What things do I need to remove?

______________________________________________

______________________________________________

______________________________________________

# Forgiving Myself as He Forgives Me

**For as high as the heavens are above the earth, so great is his love for those who fear him; as far as the east is from the west, so far has he removed our transgressions from us. – Psalm 103:11-12 (NIV)**
**I am your Creator. You were in my care even before you were born. – Isaiah 44:2 (NIV)**

Find a peaceful place to sit or lie down

Begin by taking a deep breath in, slow and intentionally
breathe in through your nose

Exhale slowly through your mouth

Continue breathing slow and deep
Go at a pace that feels natural to you

Allow the slow breaths to get the oxygen to each of your muscles
Release any tension that you have

Feel the slow breaths soothing your body and mind
Take a moment to just be

Let it soak in that your creator knew your entire story before you were born
He knew every mistake you would make
He chose to forgive you for everything you would do long before you came to earth
When you made each mistake

He forgave you
When you made each bad decision
He forgave you
When you said yes and should have said no
He forgave you
He has known every obstacle on your path before you encountered it
He has equipped you to overcome every one

Today is the day
It is the day that you forgive yourself
Follow His lead
Follow the perfect one
Follow the one true God
For every mistake
Forgive yourself
For every bad decision, you have made
Forgive yourself
For the times that you said yes and should have said no
Forgive yourself
For the times that you have procrastinated
Forgive yourself
For the times when you were disobedient
Forgive yourself

Today the slate is clean
Each day is new
Every evening give praise for the things that have gone right and ask for forgiveness for those that have not
Forgiveness from God and yourself

Today expect great things
Today expect blessings
Today expect miracles
Today expect favor

Breathe in deeply as you receive these gifts
Exhale all feelings of unworthiness

Envision yesterday's transgressions on the other side of the world
They are so far away you can no longer see them
Concentrate on the greatness of this day
Of this moment
Of this second

When you are ready
Return to your surroundings

## Journal Exercise:

1 – Continue in silence and in the vision that God has provided for you.

2 – How will you enjoy this day?

____________________________________________________________

____________________________________________________________

____________________________________________________________

3 – What can you do today to keep moving forward in the grace and mercy provided by God?

____________________________________________________________

____________________________________________________________

____________________________________________________________

4 – What situations has God restored you from?

____________________________________________________________

____________________________________________________________

____________________________________________________________

5 - Give thanks to God and wrap your arms around yourself. Hug yourself, forgive yourself, and love yourself.

# God's Vineyard

**I am the vine; you are the branches. If you remain in me and I in you, you will bear much fruit; apart from me, you can do nothing. – John 15:5 (NIV)**

Find a comfortable position
seated or lying down

Begin to focus on your breathing
Allow yourself to relax

Inhale deeply and follow your breath with your mind
Intentionally focus on where your breath is flowing

Exhale slowly and envision the release of all of your cares

Invite the Holy Spirit in with each breath
Inhale deeply to allow yourself to be filled with the Holy Spirit
Invite Him into every crevice of your body
Let the Spirit fill you up and overflow

Allow your exhales to remove anything not representative of Him
Exhale your doubts
Exhale your fears
Exhale your anxieties

Find a rhythm that works for you and continue to breathe in and out slowly

Visualize a beautiful vineyard that is going on as far as the eye can see

See the strong, thick, unbreakable vine that holds together all of the branches
Take a look at one branch
the one that has your name on it

Look at the fruit on your branch
There are beautiful plump grapes that are almost ready for harvest

Take a closer look at the branch.
Carefully note the scars and injuries that have occurred over the years due to the winds and storms
Those past scars have healed because you have stayed connected to your vine, the great I am

Peep in even closer and look at the broken branches on the ground
They are shriveled and dead
These are those who are so separated from God because they do not believe
Without the attachment to the true vine, they can do nothing

Look left and right along the vine.
Look at how each branch is able to produce fruit bountifully
There is no scarcity, only abundance
These are your brothers and sisters in Christ
All may grow abundantly in Christ without anyone having to go without
See those who will partake of the harvest

Once the grapes are full-grown
they are ready to be shared with the world
This is the goodness and the gospel that God has been feeding your soul

After being plucked empty
the branches do not die
No
In fact, this is when the vine provides the full nourishment needed to produce the next harvest
This is you continuing to grow in Christ

and God continuing to renew and restore you

What a beautiful vineyard

What a place of safety

An amazing place of peace

A haven of joy

Perfectly cared for...
As long as you are attached to the Vine

Inhale and connect
Exhale all doubt slowly

When you are ready
Slowly awaken all of your senses to your environment

## Journal Exercise:

1 - Continue in silence and in the vision that God has provided for you.

2 - Write down what harvest God has given you to share with the world.

________________________________________________

________________________________________________

________________________________________________

3 - What causes you to receive your breaks and tears in your branches?

________________________________________________

________________________________________________

________________________________________________

4 - How has he restored you after the storm(s)?

________________________________________________

________________________________________________

________________________________________________

5 - Give him your gratitude and carry this with you on this day.

# Hearing Your Cry

**Praise be to the Lord, for he has heard my cry for mercy. The Lord is my strength and my shield; my heart trusts in him, and he helps me. My heart leaps for joy, and with my song, I praise him. The Lord is the strength of his people, a fortress of salvation for his anointed one. Save you people and bless your inheritance; be their shepherd and carry them forever. – Psalms 28: 6- 9 (NIV)**

Find a place where you can get comfortable
You can get seated
You may want to lie down
Maybe you have been sitting all day, and you choose to stand
Wherever you are is completely fine

We are going to do some breathing exercises
Let's begin to center ourselves
Appreciate our current being and where we are

Take a deep breath in through your nose with a count to two
Exhale through your mouth with a count to four

As you inhale this next time
Expand your belly and let all of the air just fill it up

As you exhale through your mouth
Press your belly button back towards your back

Continue to breathe this way for a few more breaths

Think about all that is required for you to breathe
How your body is having to work together
For the air to command and expand your body
For it to leave and compress your body
How your lungs fill up, and your shoulders lift up when you inhale
How when you exhale, you may feel a little lighter
Your mind may feel a little clearer
How the breath comes in cool and leaves your body warm

Take a minute to actually just think about how you have been breathing all day without thinking about it
How your body has been perfectly designed
To do that one critical thing – taking breaths in and exhaling breaths out on it's on all day, without any help from you

As you return to your normal breathing, whatever that is for you
Think about when was the last time that you cried out to the Lord
What was it that you cried out about?
When was the moment that you knew He heard your cry?
How did He show up as the provider of mercy?

During your crying, when did you see Him as the source of your strength?
In that time, what we're all the things He shielded you from?
What was the harm He protected you from?
From yourself or others

When was the time you thought He was absent,
and when you made it to the other side, you recognized He hasn't failed me yet?

When you came to the other side of the storm
could you reflect on God being the birthplace of peace?
The authority of praise and hallelujah
The anointer of all things
Including you from your head to the soles of your feet

When you look back, do you remember Him being the multiplier of blessings>

As you move forward, knowing all the things that He has brought you through
All the times he heard your cry
Every moment he has been your strength

Will you trust him enough to be your shepherd going forward?

.

.

As we remember to praise the Lord for hearing our cries and bringing us through
Inhale goodness
Exhale all the what-if thoughts that are distracting to us

Inhale peace
Exhale all worries casting them unto the Lord

Inhale gratefulness – we have so much to be thankful for
Exhale all comparisons to others and to our pasts

Let us walk with God hand in hand
with him leading us into our new, ordained future

Take a few moments

When you are ready
Bring your mind back to where you are

## Journal Exercises:

1 – What do you need to trust God for your future plans? This could be just for tomorrow.

_______________________________________________

_______________________________________________

_______________________________________________

2 – How will you remember to praise him in difficult times?

_______________________________________________

_______________________________________________

_______________________________________________

3 – When has he heard your cry?

_______________________________________________

_______________________________________________

_______________________________________________

# I Shall Not Want

**The Lord is my shepherd; I shall not want. – Psalms 23:1 (NIV)**

Find a comfortable position
seated or lying down

Begin to focus on your breathing
Unclutter your mind

Inhale deeply, allowing your body to relax
Feel your chest filling up like a balloon as you inhale
Feel it deflating and sinking in as you exhale

Find your rhythm
One that feels completely natural to you
A rhythm of breathing in and out that allows you to feel your body relaxing
Feel your shoulders settling down
Feel the tenseness in your neck, leaving
Feel any pain or discomfort dissipating.

Ask the Holy Spirit to feel every inch of your body when you inhale
Exhale all negativity

Inhale God's peace
Exhale the world's chaos

Notice your breathing
Continue in this comfortable place

Visualize a large pasture
Filled with sheep
See the shepherd herding the flock
Feel the sense of peace the sheep have while they are cared for and protected by their shepherd

Look at the sheep
See how beautifully kept they are
They look cared for
They look fed

See the barn on the field
The shepherd provides the shelter
The sheep grow thick wool in the winter for warmth
The shepherd cuts the wool in the summer for cooling
The sheep lack nothing when they are with the shepherd
The shepherd tends to his sheep

The shepherd starts and ends their day
The shepherd provides protection during the day and night
He watches over his sheep
They do not want

You are the sheep
The Lord is your shepherd

Wanting is the lack or deficiency of something
You shall not want
As your shepherd has everything you desire
Simply ask, and you shall receive
Knock, and the door shall be answered
You have all because He created all
Let your requests be known
Watch your shepherd answer

Inhale and see your shepherd
Exhale the feeling of lacking anything

When you are ready

Focus on where you are and bring your mind to your present surroundings

# Journal Exercise:

1 - Continue in silence and in the vision that God has provided for you.

2 - Write down your requests of the Lord. Do not use the word want. Replace the word with request or desire.

_______________________________________________

_______________________________________________

_______________________________________________

3 - Visualize God granting that request in His way and in His timing. Write down or draw what you see.

4 - Give Him your thanks and praise as your request has already been granted.

# Intentionally Living in the Moment

**So do not worry, saying, 'What shall we eat?' or 'What shall we drink?' or 'What shall we wear?'[32] For the pagans run after all these things, and your heavenly Father knows that you need them. [33] But seek first his kingdom and his righteousness, and all these things will be given to you as well. [34] Therefore do not worry about tomorrow, for tomorrow will worry about itself. Each day has enough trouble of its own. Matthew 6: 31-34 (NIV)**
**But when you pray, go into your room, close the door and pray to your Father, who is unseen. Then your Father, who sees what is done in secret, will reward you. Matthew 6:6 (NIV)**
**When I am afraid, I put my trust in you. Psalm 56:3 (NIV)**
**Do not be anxious about anything, but in every situation, by prayer and petition, with thanksgiving, present your requests to God. And the peace of God, which transcends all understanding, will guard your hearts and your minds in Christ Jesus. Philippians 4:6-7 (NIV)**

Find a comfortable position
Begin to focus on your breathing
Allow yourself to relax
Follow your breath with your mind

Take a deep breath in allowing it to cleanse your body
Exhale all things unclean

Inhale and cleanse your mind
allowing the cobwebs to dissipate
Exhale releasing any distractions

Allow your mind, body, and soul to be God's resting place
Envision him planting a seed inside of you
A seed of purpose
A seed of intention
A seed of manifestation
A seed of expectation
See him digging in the dirt
Carefully placing the seed in you
Covering the seed to protect it from the damage from winds and storms
Watch him water the seed
Feel the water quenching your thirst
Feel your mind, body, and soul soaking up the water
Look at him tending to you daily
Never forgetting to check on you
Never forgetting to care for you
Never forgetting to love you
Feel his presence
Examine the sprout from the seed
Feel his patience
Back up from your view
so you can look from the sky
See how you are exactly where God has placed you
Growing how God has designed you to grow
Look for today's lesson
Look for today's blessings
Ask God for today's plans
Look for today's joys
Invite God to walk with you as you continue to grow
Knowing today, you might not be able to see the growth from yesterday
but when you look back over the season, you see much progress
God has given you what you need for this day
You are enough
You know enough

He has fully equipped you for everything that today will bring
Enjoy this day one moment, one minute, one second at a time

Rest in this space

Take slow deep breaths
Awaken all of your senses as you prepare to
Go out in love to serve the Lord

## Journal Exercises:

1 – What seeds has God planted in your life?

______________________________________________

______________________________________________

______________________________________________

2 – How can you check on the status of your seed/plant today?

______________________________________________

______________________________________________

______________________________________________

3 – Reflect on the seeds that have already sprouted

# Mindset Shifts

**Do not conform to the pattern of this world, but be transformed by the renewing of your mind. Then you will be able to test and approve what God's will is—his good, pleasing and perfect will. – Romans 12:2 (NIV)**
**"For my thoughts are not your thoughts, neither are your ways my ways," declares the Lord. "As the heavens are higher than the earth so are my ways higher than your ways and my thoughts than your thoughts." – Isaiah 55:8-9 (NIV)**

We are going to take a few deep breaths
To create awareness

Take a deep breath in through your nose for 3 counts
Hold your breath for 3 counts
Exhale slowly through your mouth 5 counts
Notice where your body is tense and where it is relaxed

Take another deep breath in through your nose for 3 counts
Hold your breath for 3 counts
Exhale slowly through your mouth 5 counts
Notice any change in your body

Last time
Inhale through your nose for 3 counts
Exhale for 5 counts
Scan your body from head to toe to see if you notice any tension
Send thoughts of relaxations to those parts

Let's take another moment to relax

Take time to just be
Just be present wherever you are
Take in your surroundings

What do you see?
(pause and take it in with your eyes)

What do you hear?
(pause and take it in with your ears)

What do you smell?
(pause and take it in with your nose)

What does this area feel like?
(pause and take it in with your body)

What are you noticing that you had not noticed before?
What thoughts are coming to your mind?

Imagine knowing that God is always taking it all in
Never missing any detail
Noticing you
Noticing your feelings
Noticing your thoughts
Noticing your gestures
Noticing your words
Noticing your actions

What are you needing to pause and notice?

Take slow deep breaths
Return fully to your surroundings
When you are ready, equip yourself to go serve the Lord

## Journal Exercise:

1 – What are you currently spending your time thinking about?

_______________________________________________

_______________________________________________

_______________________________________________

2 – What thoughts do you need to submit to the Lord and ask him to remove?

_______________________________________________

_______________________________________________

_______________________________________________

3 – What thoughts do you need to ask God to breathe life into?

_______________________________________________

_______________________________________________

_______________________________________________

4 – Are you ready to allow God to transform you from the inside out?

_______________________________________________

_______________________________________________

_______________________________________________

# New Beginnings

**In their hearts, humans plan their course, but the Lord establishes their steps. Proverbs 16:9 (NIV)**

Settle into your space
Relax and know that you are in the perfect time and space to meditate
Take in your first deep breath, slowly
Release and exhale

Explore the depth of your breath as you take in your next breath
Feel how your body responds when you exhale

Inhale again
Notice the pace that is normal to you
Continue to watch how your breathing allows your body to relax and your mind to focus
Let go of the tension in your body through taking two more breaths

Clear your mind
Know that where you are this day is exactly where God has placed you
He knew you would be in this space before you got here
He prepared this space for you before you got here
While you anticipated what it would be, He already knew
Allow His plans to become your plans
Embrace that there is growth in change
Accept that in order to become what He has designed you to be, you must change
Learn from your past
Be open to the future

Know that there is peace in walking in the steps laid before you
Walk in gratefulness, giving thanks for everything that got you here
Walk in grace, forgiving yourself for every time you forgot to consult Him
Walk in peace, knowing that regardless of your actions, He never left your side
Walk in acceptance of where you are now
Walk in love, loving Him and yourself as He loves you
Walk in faith, believing that this new space will take you further on your journey
Release all expectations you had of yourself before today
Release all anger
Release all disappointment
Release all fears
Release the people who have gone
Embrace this space
Embrace this assignment
Embrace the people who have come to assist
Embrace the lessons of the past
Explore the future
Explore the silence that creates space for you to hear God
Look to Him
Listen to Him
Ask for direction
Receive discernment
Be still
Be at peace
Just be

Receive what God has given you
Give thanks

When you are ready
Refocus on your surroundings
Reset your attitude to embrace all that is new this day

## Journal Exercise:

1 - Continue in silence and in the vision that God has provided for you.

2 - Write down what you need to forgive yourself for.

---

---

---

3 - Describe the new space you are in.

---

---

---

4 - List the people God has given to you for this new space.

---

---

---

5 - List the lessons learned.

---

---

---

6 - Write what you are currently in this space and time thankful for.

________________________________________

________________________________________

________________________________________

________________________________________

7 - Release the expectations of the future, giving God full control.

# Perfect As I am

**For as high as the heavens are above the earth, so great is his love for those who fear him; as far as the east is from the west, so far has he removed our transgressions from us. – Psalms 103:11-12**
**For you created my inmost being; you knit me together in my mother's womb. I praise you because I am fearfully and wonderfully made; your works are wonderful, I know that full well. – Psalms 139:13-14**

Please get in a comfortable position to prepare to focus on God's word today.

Let's start with our cleansing breaths

We will be breathing doing three counts for the inhale
And three counts for the exhale
Breathing in through our nose
Breathing out through our mouths
We will make an "ahh" noise when you exhale
to fully acknowledge the breath being released from your body

Take a deep cleansing breath in
Exhale, making the "ahh" sound as you breathe out
Expelling all of the air from your body

This time as you breathe in
Breathe in God's cleanliness
As you exhale

Exhale out all your sins and transgressions

As you take your third and final deep breath in
Breathe in God's word
the word of life
the word that is the water which cleanses us
Exhale all weariness
all imperfections
all doubts

Let's focus on affirming God's word
I want you to just start by thinking and repeating in your head or saying out loud
I love and accept myself as I am
as God loves and accepts me

I am uniquely designed by God
He made every single inch of me
He perfectly designed every scar and labeled them as beauty marks

God created me so He could love me
and so I could love myself
and then properly love others

I am open and able to be loved by God
Oh, how God has shown His love to me

I forgive myself as God forgives me

I separate myself from my sins
I love myself

I am exactly where God has designed for me to be
Every detail of my physical, mental and emotional being
was uniquely crafted by God for my journey
This unique vessel that I call my body
is home to the Holy Spirit
I am a place where God resides.

I choose to believe what God says about me
I am an heir
I am a lender not a borrower
I am well taken care of
I have talents
I was created for a purpose
I am at peace
I am full of joy
I am a conqueror
I can do all things through Christ
I am healed
I am loved
I am kind
I am good
I am destined for great things
I am fearfully and wonderfully made

These things I know full well!

Take a deep breath in through your nose
and inhale who God says you are

As you exhale
let go of whatever anybody on this earth has called you

On your next deep breath in
Inhale that you are God's favorite child
Exhale all negativity that you have toward yourself

As we breathe in for our last deep breath
Make room for the Holy Spirit to stay awhile
Exhale all that needs to be cleared for Him to be comfortable

## Journal Exercise:

1 – What self-talks are you having with yourself?

______________________________________________

______________________________________________

______________________________________________

2 – What parts of you do you need to pause and say I love you to?

______________________________________________

______________________________________________

______________________________________________

3 – What can you tell yourself every day that is exactly what God says about you?

______________________________________________

______________________________________________

______________________________________________

# Praying Specifically for God's Blessings

**Ask, and it will be given to you; seek, and you will find; knock, and the door will be opened to you. For everyone who asks receives; the one who seeks finds; and to the one who knocks, the door will be opened. – Matthew 7:7-8 (NIV)**
**This is the confidence we have in approaching God: that if we ask anything according to his will, he hears us. And if we know that he hears us—whatever we ask—we know that we have what we asked of him. – 1 John 5:14-15 (NIV)**
**And Jabez called on the God of Israel saying, "Oh, that You would bless me indeed, and enlarge my territory, that Your hand would be with me, and that You would keep me from evil, that I may not cause pain!" So God granted him what he requested. – 1 Chronicles 4:10 (NIV)**

Find a comfortable position
Look inwardly and begin to focus on your breathing
Allow yourself to relax
Follow your breath with your mind
Intentionally focus on where your breath is flowing
Invite the Holy Spirit in with each breath

Inhale deeply to allow yourself to be filled with the Holy Spirit
Invite him into every crevice of your body
Let the Spirit fill you up and overflow

Allow your exhales to remove anything not representative of him
Exhale your doubts
Exhale your fears
Exhale your anxieties

Breathe slowly and continue to intentionally be aware of your breathing pace
When you feel any tenseness or tightness in your body
allow yourself to breathe deeply and send it to that space
Allow your breath to enter that area
Release the tension and exhale the reason for the tension

Take a moment to clear your mind
Relax your body
Allow God to speak to you
Grant the Holy Spirit time to take over your mind
Focus on what He has for you

Envision yourself walking down the path that God has laid before you
Focus on your surroundings
Take in the details in the vision that God has shown to you
Lift up your vision to God
Give to Him what He has given to you in prayer
Ask Him to equip you specifically to accomplish the work He has for you
Receive His help
Accept His direction
Embrace His guidance
Welcome His blessings
Inhale God's plans
Exhale the plans you have made for yourself
Inhale God's will for your life
Exhale your need to be in control
Inhale God's instructions

Exhale your resistance to obey
Inhale God's knowledge

Exhale your insecurities
Remember His vision
Remember the details
Remember He created you
Remember, with Christ, all things are possible

Inhale deeply
Exhale slowly

When you are ready
Gradually raise your awareness to focus on where you actually are
Remember to pray specifically about God's plans for you
Go out and serve the Lord.

## Journal Exercise:

1 – Allow the vision to resonate within you.

________________________________________

________________________________________

________________________________________

2 – Write the specifics of what God showed you.

________________________________________

________________________________________

________________________________________

3 – Lift your prayers to God.

________________________________________

________________________________________

________________________________________

# Reminding Myself What God Says About Me

I am his child. Reference – **1 John 3:1**
God knew me before he formed me in my mother's womb. Reference – **Jeremiah 1:5**
I am meant to inherit from God. Reference - **Romans 8:17**
I am the head and not the tail. Reference – **Deuteronomy 28:13**
I am forgiven. Reference – **Ephesians 1:7**
I am clothed in strength and dignity. Reference – **Proverbs 31:25**
I am fearfully and wonderfully made. Reference – **Psalms 139:14**
I am altogether beautiful. Reference – **Song of Songs 4:7**
I am more precious than rubies. Reference – **Proverbs 3:15**
I have everything I need to live the life God has designed for me. Reference - **2 Peter 1:3-4**

Take a moment to settle in
Get comfortable
Wiggle your toes
Open and close your hands
Move your fingers around
Take in your surroundings
Just become aware of where you are
If you are able, for a moment, close your eyes as your awareness increases

When the days get long and seem to run together
It is best to be obedient to God and slow down
Take a moment to breathe
To actually acknowledge the thing that you do so naturally and take for granted
Pause and notice what is happening this very moment

Choose the good portion of the day as Mary did (**Luke 10:38-42**)

In the pause....remind yourself who you are
Whose you are
You are a child of God
One created purposefully and intentionally by the Lord
An heir to the throne
A leader and not a follower
One forgiven for all mistakes of the past
Rising each day with strength and dignity
Your designer label says fearfully and wonderfully made
A masterpiece that is beautiful
A precious thing more exquisite than rubies
Your recipe card says when mixed with the Holy Spirit, submission, and obedience, you are complete
God has everything under control

You are free to let go

Yes, do what you can
Let God do the rest
Take a moment to just be

Take a deep breath in
Exhale slowly

Once more
Take a deep breath in
Exhale slowly

## Journal Exercise:

1 - Take a few moments to create some affirmations; your "I am...." Statements

______________________________________________

______________________________________________

______________________________________________

2 - What do you need to tell yourself?

______________________________________________

______________________________________________

______________________________________________

3 - What do you want or need to hear more of?

______________________________________________

______________________________________________

______________________________________________

**Next Steps:**

- Put your affirmations up where you will see them
- Read them everyday
- Say them everyday
- Until you believe it

# Saved From Distress

**Then they cried to the Lord in their trouble, and he saved them from their distress. – Psalms 107:13 (NIV)**

Find a comfortable space
A space that will allow you to be still for a moment
A place that is not too distracting
Where you can center yourself and your mind on God
I want to remind you that it is okay for your mind to wander
It is okay for it to have thoughts pass through as we do this
Acknowledge the thought and let it pass
If you can or are able, re-center your mind on our scripture

Take a few centering breaths to become fully present in the moment with whatever it is that this scripture speaks to you

Take a deep breath in through your nose
Expand your lungs
Exhale through your mouth
Press the front of your body towards your back

Inhale through your nose
Exhale all impurities, all un-pure thoughts, and all distractions

Inhale in awareness
Concentrate on where your breath is going and how your body is feeling
As you exhale, release all tensions
Allow your body to relax like a rag doll

Steady your breath to a normal pattern

Think about the word today
When was the last time you cried to the Lord
Were you experiencing tears of joy and saying, thank you Jesus
Were you experiencing moments of pain and saying, save me Jesus
Were you going through times of uncertainty and helplessness and saying, help me Jesus
Were you going through time of loss and saying, hold me Jesus
Was it a time of just too much and you couldn't even identify the feeling, and you just said, take the wheel Jesus

Was the cry out cleansing to your soul
Were the tears refreshing to your body
When you cried out to the Lord, did you feel as if you had given him all of you
After your crying out to the Lord, do you remember how you felt
Can you remember finding the reset button and remembering that he was your foundation
Can you remember thinking even later, I don't know why I didn't call on him sooner
Were you saying fix it Jesus, fix it

When you look back, were you able to see that he was fixing it all along
That He was waiting for you to ask him for help
To ask Him for wisdom
To ask Him for guidance
To ask Him for protection
To ask Him for peace
To ask Him for a steady mind
To ask Him for faithfulness, that is unshaken
To ask Him for joy
To ask Him for a grateful heart
To ask Him to see things as He sees them

When was the last time you cried out to the Lord?
When was the last time He heard you and save you?
What is He saving you from right now?

Inhale God's grace
Exhale every doubt or fear that he will ever forsake you

Inhale God's peace
Exhale...shaking off everything that you have said to yourself to make you doubt that the peace is still there

Inhale again for clear vision
Exhale all cloudiness, all fogginess, all haze

Sit with the Holy Spirit for a moment

When you are ready bring your mind back to your current surroundings

## Journal Entry:

1 – What has God saved you from?

______________________________________________

______________________________________________

______________________________________________

2 – Who were you before you cried out to the Lord?

______________________________________________

______________________________________________

______________________________________________

3 – How were you different after crying out to the Lord?

______________________________________________

______________________________________________

______________________________________________

> *Faith doesn't always mean that God changes your situation. Sometimes it means that he changes you*
>
> . – Author unknown

# She Will Not Fail

**God is within her, she will not fail; God will help her at the break of day. – Psalms 46:5 (NIV)**

Breathe in through your nose for a count of 2
Breath out through your mouth for a count of 4

As you breathe in this time
allow the Holy Spirit to be welcomed into this place

As you exhale
cast all of your anxieties on the Lord

Breathe in once more to clear your mind
Exhale all distractions

Visualize you doing a task that God has led you to do
Visualize how large the task seems when you first get started
The questions that come to your head
How will I do it?
How will I get it done?
Is it too much for me?

I want you to see God walking up behind you
Coming beside you and taking your hand
Whispering to you, he will provide all the plans
All you have to do is listen and be obedient

Visualize him breaking down the task into your first step
And you lifting your foot and moving forward

He is there to hold you
He is there to steady you
He is there to ensure that you won't fail

The first step is successful
You're smiling
You're radiant
You're beaming
Ready to take the second step
He helps you with that
You get into a rhythm
Your rhythm is such that it feels natural
That you almost think that you are doing it by yourself

Then you reach a stumbling block, an obstacle
Phase II seems just as high a mountain as Phase I
You look around only to be comforted that your Father is still by your side
He repeats the steps of allowing you to continue on His path
Step by step
He does this in your home
He does this at your job
He does this in your business
He does this with your children
He does this with your friendships
He does this with your relationships of significance

When he emerges at the break of day
All is well
You are steady
You are unshifting
Your feet are planted firmly
Because He is within you
He resides within you
He provides everything you need to do what He has placed you on this earth to do
He gives you the courage
He provides for you the wisdom
He gives you the tools and resources

To take one step at a time

Imagine his face shining upon you
When you seek him and take the first step

How does it feel
To see the face of the Lord shining down upon you

He waits for us to cry out like Jabez
Oh Lord that you would bless me
And enlarge my territory
Let your hand be with me
And keep me from harm
So that I would be free from pain
God granted the request

He is within us
We shall not fail
God will help us at the break of day

Take a deep breath in
Exhale slowly

Inhale with the expectation to hear from God
Exhale all other voices
We can hear no one but the voice of God

Inhale and surrender to His will
Exhale all things that are fighting His way

Inhale obedience
Exhale all stubbornness

When you are ready
Bring your full awareness back to your current surroundings

## Journal Exercise:

1 – What has God asked you to do?

______________________________________________

______________________________________________

______________________________________________

2 – What is preventing you from acting on it?

______________________________________________

______________________________________________

______________________________________________

3 – Ask God to provide you with everything you need to be successful and bring him the glory. What do you feel you need to do the task He has given to you?

______________________________________________

______________________________________________

______________________________________________

4 – What is the first step? Do just that.

______________________________________________

______________________________________________

______________________________________________

# What's Your Next Miracle?

**He performs wonders that cannot be fathomed, miracles that cannot be counted. – Job 5:9 (NIV)**
**You are the God who performs miracles; you display your power among the peoples. – Psalms 77:14 (NIV)**

I invite you to get in a space that will invite the Holy Spirit to penetrate your heart and mind
Sitting up
Lying down
Standing up
Stretched out on your belly
Whatever position is most comfortable to you

I invite you to begin to slow down
I invite you to take some long breaths

Taking in a deep breath through your nose
Exhale through your mouth

Inhale again deeply through your nose
Allow your body to expand and fill up with air
Exhale through your mouth
Twice as slow
Allowing everything to decompress
Allow all the air to get completely out of your system

Take in a third cleansing breath
Breathing in God's goodness, pureness, wholesomeness

Exhale through our mouth, all impurities, all things that are not of our God

Take a moment to return to your normal breathing pattern
Your resting pattern

As you think about the word
Think about, what is a miracle?

Miracles are those things that are happening around us
that are beyond our understanding and comprehension

Miracles are those things that when people ask us,
how did that happen, we have absolutely no idea, and all we can say is "but God"

Miracles are happening every second
every minute
every hour of each day

Miracles are the beginning of our lives
Human birth is a miracle
It is when God plants a seed inside of a woman
We go from egg and sperm
to a fetus
and grow into a newborn

Miracles are when both the mother and the child come out of birth

Miracles are the fact that we are breathing without thinking about it

Miracles are our minds thinking without telling them to do so

Think of the things that you probably think are routine
What about the things that you do automatically
in your mind
all by yourself without trying
What about those things are really God's miracle?

How can you become more aware of the everyday miracles that God is producing continuously in your life?

When you woke up this morning...God's miracle

When you stood up to walk and carry these heavy bodies on these two feet that are disproportionate to our bodies....God's miracle

When we use our talent or gift....God's miracle

When we tune in and hear the voice of the Holy Spirit...God's miracle

Everyday miracles are happening all around us
They are scattered all over our paths
What can we do to not trip over those miracles?
To open our eyes and see them
Acknowledge them
Be grateful for them
As we notice the small ones, we are reassured
We are more connected
We are repurposed
Our mind shifts to remember that his miracles cannot be counted
They are more than the huge, in between ones that we look for humanly

What is your next miracle?

I invite you to take a deep breath in
Exhale through your mouth
Ask God to center your mind

Inhale again through your nose
Exhale through your mouth
Have God cleanse your heart

Inhale through your nose
Out through your mouth
Welcome God's presence to stay and reside within you

And point out the everyday miracles

When you are ready
Return to your surroundings

## Journal Exercise:

1 – How do you define "miracle"?

___

___

___

2 – Over your lifetime, what miracles have you experienced?

___

___

___

3 – What miracles are you currently tripping over/overlooking?

___

___

___

# You Are A Visionary

**Blessed is she who has believed that the Lord would fulfill his promises to her. – Luke 1:45 (NIV)**
**..he said, "When there is a prophet among you, I, the Lord, reveal myself to them in visions; I speak to them in dreams." – Numbers 12:6 (NIV)**

Take a moment to be settled
Get comfortable

Begin to breathe in for 2 counts
Breathe out for 4 counts

Breathe in slowly
Breathe out and release the tensions of the day

As you are breathing, take a moment to slow down
Notice the air coming into your body
Notice how it is cool coming in and warm going out
Take a moment to appreciate each breath

Continue breathing in and out in a slow and natural rhythm
Ask God to enter your mind
Allow him to control your thoughts
Remove the clutter

Picture a blank canvas
Ask God to paint for you a picture of his promises
Promises of protection
Promises of being a provider for strength and courage

Promises to watch over you
Promises to always be with you and never leave you
Promises to guide you
Promises to give you wisdom
Promises that his word will never change
Promises to defend you at all times
Promises that no matter what it looks like, he is working everything out for your good
Promises to shield you
Promises to plan your life from beginning to the very end
Promises that every morning we will have fresh mercy
Promises to carry each and every one of our burdens
Promises of healing
Promises of providing favor
Promises to be a peace maker
Promises to be a rainmaker of blessings
Promises to be a comforter

Look at your canvas
What has God spoken specifically to you about

God is the creator of visions
He gives you visions
He makes you a visionary
What is the vision that God has given to you?

Press in
Listen for God to speak
Hear God sharing his thoughts with you
Listen to the ideas that he has provided to you
See his vision

Look at the canvas
What do you see?
The canvas contains God's promises designed specifically for you
God's communication with you becomes clearer as you draw nearer to him
Walk towards God so you can see clearer
What is on the canvas now that you couldn't see before?

Look closely
Take in every single detail

Ask God to imprint this canvas on your heart and mind
Ask him to stand with you, beside you, in you as you soak it all up

Breathe in the vision
Exhale all distractions

Breathe in God's promises
Release all doubts

Receive and believe God's promises
For YOU

## Journal Exercise:

1 - Write down or draw the vision that God gave you in as much detail as possible.

Next Steps:

- Trust and believe that God will fulfill his promises
- Wait on the direction from the Lord
- Once provided, do what he says quickly.

# You Are Courageous

**Be strong and courageous. Do not be afraid and terrified because of them. For the Lord your God goes with you. He will never leave you nor forsake you. – Deuteronomy 31:6**

**Have I not commanded you? Be strong and courageous. Do not be afraid. Do not be discouraged. For the Lord your God will be with you wherever you go. – Joshua 1:9**

Please find a space where you are settled in
You can be standing, seated, laying down
Wherever is peaceful for you

Invite God in and do as he has commanded us to do
Meditate on his word
Relax your mind

Before we get into our deep breathing
I want to provide you with 2 definitions of courage
1 – Courage is the ability to do something that frightens one
2 – Courage is strength in the face of pain or grief

We are going to breathe in for 3 counts and breathe out for 3 counts

As we breathe in, breathe in courage
As we exhale, exhale fear

On the second inhale, we are seeking to inhale courage again
As we exhale, we are exhaling disobedience

On the third breath in, we are inhaling courage
As we breathe out, we are exhaling hesitation

Take two more deep breaths
Inhaling courage each time
And exhaling whatever is in you that should not be

Open your heart and mind to allow God to settle in
As we meditate on being strong and courageous
Let's go on a guided reflection

Where have you been during your lifetime?

Specifically, what obstacles have you faced?

What things have you gone through?

Think for a moment about how you made it to the other side.

In reflecting, I am asking you to remember the times of courage
The time perhaps when you spoke in front of a crowd, and you were nervous
The time you left what felt like a comfortable relationship, but it just didn't feel right, and you were going to be alone
The time when you talked to a complete stranger, even though others may have seen that as foolish
That time you signed up to take that task, and all of a sudden, it felt way too big
That time you took a leap of faith and acted on what God said without knowing the reason or the outcome

Courage

Courage is the first step in showing others love
In being vulnerable
It takes courage to be kind
It takes courage to be good and seek goodness

Courage is the foundation of faithfulness
It takes courage to forgive
It takes courage to have self-control

Courage is making a good decision in troubling times
Courage is trusting God
When courage shows up, don't just say you trust God
Take the first step
And trust God to provide whatever is needed
The words
The wisdom
The actions
The decisions
And the next step

Courage is how we become unstuck
Courage is how we move forward
As we move forward
And take one step
We are that much closer to becoming what God designed us to be
Moment by moment
Minute by minute
Second by second
Being strong and courageous

Take a deep breath and inhale courage
Exhale fear

Inhale courage
Exhale disobedience

Inhale courage
Exhale hesitation

I invite you to be strong and courageous.
By just taking one step

When you are ready
Refocus on your surroundings

## Journal Exercise:

1 – What is God asking you to do?

2 – What is the first piece of the task?

Remember what God has already brought you through, and trust him as you do the first piece. He will provide the rest of whatever is needed on the journey. He is waiting on you.

> Fun fact – depending on the version of the bible that you read, God tells us 6 – 10 times to be "be strong and courageous"

# You Are Enough

**But he said to me, "My grace is sufficient for you, for my power is made perfect in weakness." Therefore, I will boast all the more gladly about my weaknesses so that Christ's power may rest on me. – 2 Corinthians 12:9 NIV**
**She did what she could. – Mark 14:8 NIV**

Find a comfortable place
Wherever you can to be still for a moment
Wherever you can clear your mind

Breathe in, taking a moment to declutter your mind
Breathe out, exhaling all distractions

Breathe in and out, slowly finding a rhythm where you can relax
Repeat this 3-5 times

Think about a time when something was too much
The situation seemed too big
The mountain seemed too high to climb
The pain was too much to bear
The deadline was too soon to meet
The problem was too hard to solve
How did you feel?

Did you have some anxiety?
Did you feel inadequate?
Did you feel ill-equipped?
Did you feel like it was more than what you could do?
Did it feel impossible?

Think about that same time again
At what point did you ask God for help?
Before you started?
Right when you began?
When you realized that you would not be able to do this alone?

Did you tell your God about your weaknesses?
Did you tell your God about your imperfections?
Did you tell your God about your incapability to do this thing without Him?
What happened when you called on Him?
What happened when you trusted Him?
What happened when you did what you could and called on Him to do the rest?

Our God made you perfectly imperfect
He made you to be enough
He made you to submit and obey Him
He made you to depend on Him
He made you to love you
He made you for you to love Him
He made you so that you would call on Him in every circumstance
He made you to do the impossible so that you could give Him all of the Glory
He made you to trust Him – in all thing big and small
He made you to have you invite Him into every single moment of your day
He made you to be intentional about knowing Him
He made you to do what you can
He made you to do your best and allow him and know that he will do the rest
He made you to be enough

Inhale who you are
Exhale all the worldly opinions
Inhale in God's word
Release all disbelief

When you are ready
Refocus on your surroundings

## Journal Entries:

1 – What do you normally do when you face circumstances that feel like too much?

________________________________________

________________________________________

________________________________________

2 – What can you do to bring God into those situations sooner?

________________________________________

________________________________________

________________________________________

3 – How can you trust God more?

________________________________________

________________________________________

________________________________________

# Thank You

Thank you so much for entrusting me with such an intimate process. I hope you have enjoyed this mediation journey. During this time, I trust that you had time to draw closer to God, do some self-reflection and introspection and gain a sense of peace and clarity as well. Remember, it is important to continue to take time to breathe each day, even if only for a few moments.

Feel free to come back to the meditations in the book as often as you wish. You may find the same meditation provides you with different insights each time you do them. I learned my answers to the journal questions changed over the years and because I keep notes I am able to track my progress and give thanks to God for continuing to work on me.

I welcome any feedback, thoughts or comments you have. If you want to meditate with me or invite me to your retreats or gatherings, I can be reached at info@practicalskillsu.com.

Wishing you peace, health, and abundance in everything you do!

Made in the USA
Monee, IL
20 April 2021

65216719R00056